lonesome cities

Books by Rod McKuen

And Autumn Came
Stanyan Street & Other Sorrows
Listen To The Warm
Lonesome Cities
Twelve Years Of Christmas
In Someone's Shadow
New Ballads
Caught In The Quiet
Fields Of Wonder
With Love . . .

lonesome cities

ROD McKUEN

MICHAEL JOSEPH LONDON

First published in Great Britain by
MICHAEL JOSEPH LTD
52 Bedford Square
London, W.C.1
1971

7181 0863 9

Printed in Great Britain by
Hollen Street Press Ltd at Slough
and bound by James Burn at Esher, Surrey

This is a book for Ed Habib,
who traveled some of the towns with me
as my road manager and friend.

CONTENTS

1   **PROLOGUE: The Art of Catching Trains**

13   **San Francisco**
Morning, one
Morning, two
Morning, three

23   **Paris**
One
Two
Three

29   **Venice**

35   **London**
Berkeley
Hotel Room

41   **Cheyenne**
Cowboys, one
Cowboys, two
Cowboys, three
Indians

49   **Los Angeles**
Boat Ride
Heroes
For My Son
Plan
An Outstretched Hand

57   **Tokyo**
     Fish Kites
     Baggage
     Suburb

63   **Gstaad**
     New Year's Eve
     Concerto for Four Hands

69   **Notes from a Letter to Ellen**
     Manhattan Beach
     Portuguese Bend
     El Monte
     Seattle
     Atlantic Crossing
     For Bimby
     Cannes

89   **Thirteen Songs**
     The Single Man
     I'll Never Be Alone
     Where Are We Now?
     Sommerset
     Silence Is Golden
     Blessings in Shades of Green
     The Word Before Good-bye
     Some of Them Fall
     It's Raining
     The Last of the Wine
     I've Saved the Summer
     Rusting in the Rain
     Lonesome Cities

Prologue

The Art of Catching Trains

1

I came through the clothesline maze
                of childhood
in basketball shoes.
Up from the cracked cement of sidewalks.
Long hair blowing in the breeze
from barber-college haircuts.
I moved into the country
knowing love better than long division.

Tricking out with women twice my age
we acted out our own French postcards.
Dr. Jekyll in the schoolyard.
Mr. Hyde behind the barn.

After school the trains,
Their whistles known by heart.
Pennies flattened on a rail
and dresser drawers with matchbooks
         from every northern town—
thrown by unknown travelers
who never waved back.

I knew the U.P. right of way so well
that gandy dancers called me toe-head
till they learned my name
and engineers would sometimes whistle
              down the scale
         on seeing my arm raised.

Baseball's just a sissy game
to anyone who's waved at passing trains.

You learn from hobos
the art of catching trains.
Locomotives slow at trestles
and whistle stops
            to hook the mail.

Diving through an open boxcar
you lie there till your breath comes back.
Then standing in the doorway you're the king
as crowns of hills and towns go by
and nighttime eats the summer up
and spits the stars across the sky.

How did I come to know
so many lonesome cities
with only pennies in my pockets?
I smiled a lot
        and rode a lot of trains
and got to know conductors
and railroad bulls by name.
From Alamo to Naples is a ride
that took me nearly twenty years.
But here I am,
my cardboard suitcase traded in for leather.

2

Now a traveler
under the gray-black winter sky
moving down the mountain by torchlight,
I've come to find
a gathering of eagles.
Not for the sake of mingling
           with the great birds,
but only to justify
a thousand streets walked end to end.
Ten thousand evenings spent listening
to the small sounds of the night
in station after station.

Not every town in Switzerland
has a golden *Gondelbahn,*
but there are other ways
to climb the hills
and reach the lonesome cities
                of the world.

Riding friendly bodies
you can inch your way to Heaven
let alone the far side of the room
and who'd deny that brushing elbows
                in certain streets
has not produced for every man
at least one vision of Atlantis.

For me old habits don't break easily
                I wait for trains.

Sometimes I feel I've always been
just passing through.
On my way away, or toward.
Shouting allelulias in an unseen choir
or whispering fados down beneath my breath
            waiting for an echo
not an answer.
Everybody has the answers
or they'll make them up
                    for you.

Just once I'd like to hear
a brand-new question.

What about the trains you ride
do they go fast or slow
would I recognize your face
clacking past the poplar trees
if I were stationed on some hill?

If I did I'd know you
by the look of nothing in your eyes
the kindred look that travelers have
the one that says a tentative hello.

If while riding down the rails
you see a boy in overalls
along the railroad right of way
                    wave as you go by.
Signal with a frown
you too are going down
                    the same road.

Small boys need encouragement
the freight trains in their minds
will only take them just so far.
Be kind
    for small boys need to grow.

San Francisco

MORNING, One

It is the morning of our love
our sighs are all snow-silver white
and clean as breakfast napkins.

We'll go gently then
        into the day
keeping the morning in mind,
for too soon the sun
eats up the shadows.

Come see the pussy willows grow,
do up your hair and nothing else.
We'll buy up all the butterflies
            and make the morning last.

MORNING, Two

We sleep well together
in nobody's world
but our own.
       A Monday-sleep.
A stomach-to-stomach safety sleep,
that wraps us in each other
and takes us from ourselves.

The parish priest
worried over my soul when I was younger.
We go to church one day a week
to take us from our selfish selves
       he used to say.
It was the best excuse I ever heard
   for organized believing.

Who would have thought religion
Could be so simple.

MORNING, Three

I rise up singing from your belly,
like some glad keeper of the palace swans
content to serve your navel
as an acolyte would serve his unseen god
and take your perspiration as communion.

Rolling now together in our bedroom world
we'll map out elbows and each other's backs.
There are some parts of you
           that have no highways.
Hairy forests cover even well-worn paths
but every forest has its own surprises
and the hiker coming through the glade
can only marvel as Columbus would
at sailing past the old world's edge.

Volcanos now erupting
down below your belly
are saying that your breakfast
            is past due.
Orange juice then
or coffee and brioche
or one more gentle feeding mouth to mouth.
I'll wash the sleep from off your eyes
and rub myself in shoulder smells
and touch your back from top to bottom
too happy to remember other backs.

Back into the forest
to lose myself and find myself
and fall back dying once again
in your arms only,
and wound your breasts
with new hands one more time.

The day gone or going
we'll bus from room to room
and I'll protest the eyes of furniture
              or flowers
or anything that looks at you but me.

I like the bed unmade.
It smells like each of us in turn
and each of us together.
I know the telephone
is crying for attention.
A *minute more*.
It's not the telephone at all
but celebrations of a brand-new kind
ringing from the watching walls.

Look at us.
It doesn't matter any more.
You like my weight and too fast breath
          and smile in disbelief.
I'm smiling too.
I've yet to think of last week's friend
or Julie Andrews' face.

Paris

ONE

You turn a corner and things change.
Like wrinkles changing into dimples
and nighttime changing into day.
And love changing back again
to whatever it was before it came.

Let it be.
It is a kind of something
we don't know much about,
Like Pere Nöel or magic.
Don't even dwell on the good times—
they only make you think.

TWO

I went back to look for you.
        Not understanding the language of hello
I thought I'd speak it just the same.
I bathed.
left the window open
    and one light on.
The heat was off
and as we warmed each other
You made up
for all those dark indifferent backs
that turned from me these many months.

The room sat waiting
premeditated as a concierge's smile.

In the lobby
there were some roses on a table
I looked at them so long
I thought the buds had drained
the color from my face.
Finally I went up the stairs
to bed alone.

THREE

I've drawn your face
on tablecloths across the country.
Tracing your smile
with my index finger,
making your hair just so.
Till now you're more
what I want you to be
than what you are.

I can paint your eyes and say
this is where I lived
for twenty minutes and more.

I order grapefruit
and pay for ruined napkins.
And between the morning and the evening
I draw your face a little fainter every day.

Venice

The birds waited
on the balcony this morning
for you to feed them our leftover croissants.
Ignoring me you ignored the pigeons too
and they chattered all day long.

We came to Venice so you might find the sun.
                                        Did you?
Was it in an alleyway or Harry's Bar?
Did it move beneath a gondolier's wide hat?
And did the sun while eating up your skin
chew away the last of us as well?

The sun is a movable target.
It stayed with me in St. Mark's Square
and followed you to Lido Beach as well.

My hair is almost white from lying in the sun.
I'm tired of being next to you
just to engineer a tan.
I'd be the same man pale.

Tomorrow Cannes.
Another sun that ends when I go home.
                Then I'll be by myself
                        in friendly shade.

I cannot excite you
with motor trips or first-class airplane rides
or voyages where French cuisine abounds.
You live in worlds I'll never know
the stranger's smile
            the journeyman's approving glance
a night remembered once
that sends you to the other side of bed
and keeps you there.

I tried by buying you a golden coin
a trip around the world and back
a passage to my secret self.
They were not enough.

I'll never be so rich or influential
to excite you with myself.

I didn't run my whole long life
        toward this moment
                to meet this time
to be told by your indifferent eyes
that I am not as handsome as I hoped I was.
                A mirror could have told me that.

I came in hope of finding
        a way to expand my own reflection
to make it more than what it is.
If I must go away with less
fortify me with your smile.

The journey back
is longer than the forward run.

London

_for Michael Young
and Jeffrey Gardiner_

BERKELEY

The anemones wilting on the mantlepiece
the bitter brigade of umbrellas
marching past the window
queuing down the corner for the bus
and me without a sleeping pill
                waiting for what?
The rain to stop?
Inspiration to begin?
London to be kind to me?

I do not think Godot will come tonight.
But all the same I leave the window open.

HOTEL ROOM

The hotel room is four flights up
just high enough for me to see
the tops of heads I'll never touch.
Brown hair, yellow hair,
hatless heads and heads with hats.
People alone, people together
watched by my sniper's eye—
poised to drop invisible love bombs

Cheyenne

COWBOYS, One

Brave
they straddle the animals,
hearts racing before the pistol sings
then leaping from the chute
man and animal as one
wedded groin to back.

One small moment in the air
and then the mud.

Hats retrieved
Levis dusted
back to the bull pen
to wait the next event.

Sundays choirboys
in cowboy hats.

COWBOYS, Two

Huddled in the pits
below the grandstand
or lining at the telephone
to call home victories
they make a gentle picture.
Their billfolds bulging just enough
to make another entrance fee.

Next week Omaha or Dallas.
San Antonio is yet to come.
And now the Cheyenne autumn
     like a golden thread
ties them till the weekend's done.

COWBOYS, Three

They wade through beer cans
piled ankle high in gutters—
the rodeo has moved
    down from the fairground
to the town
and every hotel door's ajar.
Better than the Mardi Gras.
The nights are longer than Alaska now
until the main event begins
        another afternoon.

But after all the Main Event is still to be
a cowboy
For ten minutes or ten years, it's all the same.
You don't forget the Levis
        hugging you all day
and Stetson hats checked in passing windows
    cocked a certain way.

Some years later
when the bellies
flow over the belt loops
there's always mental photographs.
   Here the hero in midair.
Now the Dallas hotel room.
Now again the gaping tourists
licking off the Levis with their eyes.
Photographs of feeling
   mirrored in the mind.

INDIANS

Comes now the summer of unwinding.
The goldenrod riot on the river bank
and all the frogs sing new songs
        as the world is emptied out
                    to suit the needs of man.
And our wants grow stronger every day.
Thicket beds and flower rooms no longer do.
Sunshine is not enough
            though it should be.

The Indian paintbrush growing in the hills
reminds us that we can't buy back the buffalo.
So we build another tower
        and fence another red man off.
And with all the factories built
and all the black and red men safely fenced away
we'll die a total white
with nothing but the gray of buildings for a shadow.

Los Angeles

BOAT RIDE

I surprised you
      eating a yawn.
Perhaps the boredom
    drove us to each other.
God knows that room was full of tired smiles.

You were wearing Texas on your tongue
    drawling *hello*
        and *hello* again
and *hello* again.

I've known your arms in public now
      over the water
  under the moon.
Another time,
Another place,
privately *hello* again.

HEROES

Salute the G.I. coming from the green
brandishing the ears and tail
   of his yellow enemy.
Hurry or you'll miss it on T.V.

And on the further bank
   the white stud lying in the ditch
the golden bridgework missing
from his gaping bloody mouth.

The media
has canonized the white man.
The far left claims the hero
   has a yellow tint.

But all the real heroes
   stay in used-car lots
selling bright red autos
with shoulder safety belts
for the freeway war at home.

FOR MY SON

Watching children grow
is like threatening the ivy
        to climb the garden wall.
You wait for it to happen
you hurry it along with love.
But still you're disappointed
at giving someone life enough
to walk off on their own
and not be carried in your arms.
    You never turn your back—not once,
and yet one day they've grown apart
                            or taller.
        It's all the same.

Polly put the kettle on we'll all have tea.
Giving love to children
has made us older overnight.

PLAN

My cousin Max is being married
                    on a quiz show.
He is getting a Westinghouse refrigerator
                    a Singer sewing machine
a set of furniture from Sears and Roebuck
            an ant farm
        a General Electric toaster
and a girl.

It is not enough.
He expects babies and happiness
good times and money
and a government that wars on war.

My cousin Max expects too much.

AN OUTSTRETCHED HAND

for Jay Allen

Each of us was made by God
and some of us grew tall.
Others stood out in the wind
their branches bent and fell.
Those of us who walk in light
must help the ones in darkness up.
For that's what life is all about
and love is all there is to life.

Each of us was made by God
beautiful in His mind's eye.
Those of us that turned out sound
should look across our shoulders once
and help the weak ones to their feet.

It only takes an outstretched hand.

Tokyo

FISH KITES

We'll go to Tachikawa for the weekend.
As we slip by the fields
we'll see a hundred shades of green
run along the window of the train.

Boys' Day
and all the fish kites
will be flying from the rooftops.

Sink down into my lap and sleep.
Untroubled sleep of those who know
that weekends only last two days
and have an address list
of long-forgotten names
to prove it.

BAGGAGE

The year was only
one long noisy day
that never knew a quiet night.
                        Your grin
(once strong as any shoulder)
disappearing in so many crowded rooms
each time I thought I'd found your face again
hardly helped at all.

I suppose it was a glad adventure
                however quickly gone.
Still leave me your address
so I won't have to stand in line
                at American Express.

SUBURB

The wind moves down the mountain
blowing petals in the temple yard.
A palace long deserted
      decaying like the country
never bothers to look up.

No smoke rises
from those electric chimneys now
where pine wood once sent perfume
      floating on the town.

The Buddha's smile is cracked
but still he smiles.
He's seen the centuries of worker ants
bringing progress to the countryside
by chopping down the trees
and folding down the hills
to make them flat as California.

Gstaad

for Tom Holtz

NEW YEAR'S EVE

The snow this morning
perches on the bare branches of trees
        like cherry blossoms.
White confetti picked up by the wind
falling on the path below the window
dying under footfall
    the way the old year dies tomorrow.

Prisoner of a hundred Sundays
that I never made.
Product of the times
I had no choice about.
I am like the old year dying in the snow.
Not to rise again until the ground goes green.

I have not seen those faces I need yet
          though I know they're here.
In the town
     coming down the slopes to the valley
behind the curtains in the next room,
just beyond the rain they wait.
Needing as I need.

In the village this morning
it was raining on The Burtons.
In Gstaad it rains on celebrities
and celebrants alike.
I am given to celebrations
     so there's hope.

CONCERTO FOR FOUR HANDS

Those waiting shadows
have always come along in time
to save me from the mischief of myself.
Now in this snow-baroque winter
            this Telemann time of Empty
do some shadows not yet formed
conspire to fill my empty mattress,
my too wide room?

Come soon then
for I am growing tired of Telemann
I could use some Bach.

Notes from a Letter to Ellen

MANHATTAN BEACH

I've taken a house at Manhattan Beach
working the summer into a book.

Eddie came last weekend
and brought two girls and some books.
The girls were pretty but the books stayed longer
and now they menace me stacked up on the floor
        staring back in unread smugness.

Otherwise I've had no visitors.

It's hard to sleep
though I try breathing with the waves.
It only makes me think
of our own breathing counterpoint.

At first I missed the traffic
    then the telephone.
Finally I call back
a hundred more familiar rooms
and sink down past the pillow's eye.
It's made me think I ought to try and buy
songs and safe surroundings I know best
and keep them in a half-packed suitcase
for sojourns such as these.

Katie keeps me company
and brings me back fantastic things
from her daily runs along the beach.
A weathered stick
            a bottle with no note
                        assorted other dogs.
She has, I fear, bad taste in canine friends
(the kind you say I've lately had in people).

Still lying by my bed at night
she smells like all the seas I've known
and that's a comfort to the sailor in me.

Will I see Capri again?
Hydra's just a name now
though once the big boats
            filled the harbor
and young Greeks made me dance,
while up above the Suco-Suco
a boy of fifteen stretched himself
and caught me thinking ten years back
regretting not the gone-forever mornings
but wondering only how I'd live
            another afternoon.

I nearly died that August.
Some fever made of lamb no doubt
or nightly walks along the harbor.
I stayed alive on summer squash and Coca-Cola
                and wrote no songs.

No letters came that summer either
and I was down to eighty drachma
when I left the island.

Still I would go back
but not to Athens with its tear gas for the masses
                and bayonets—
            the buckshot of the upper classes.

Naples is the asshole of the world
        (ah, but there's Capri).
Majorca still has buggy rides
that take you to the sea.

Outside Katie's barking on the beach.
She's found a seal
        that wants to play.

PORTUGUESE BEND

There on the winter beach
the fishermen coming home at dark
unbuckling their sandals
and loosening the smiles
they save for comrades only
replacing them with the kind
they give their children.

I'm told that California
sits upon a shelf
and one October day
an earthquake will send it rumbling
to the bottom of the sea.

I won't be there.
I'll be out with the fishermen
where the water's safe
for everything but fish.

EL MONTE

I probably will never see El Monte on a Sunday
or El Segundo washed by winter rain.
I never knew these towns existed—if they do,
outside of the obituary page that states
how many boys came home today in boxes made of steel.
I'm well aware that some have died from Chicago too
but it's the new El Nowhere towns
          I think about this morning
and young men that the whole town knew.

Today some children running down the hill
        were shouting out *the war is over*.
They must have had some private war of words in mind.
Not the one I'm paying for
the one that's killing off the boys I see on airplane rides
staring into space in search of El Dorado.
Sometimes I ask them where they're from,
El Paso is the answer or El Monte.

And so they take the tinsel from our lives
on airplane rides across the sea
and like the silver in our dimes
it won't come back
   until we question *why*.

El Monte's just ten minutes from L.A.
to some I'm told
 it seems like El Dorado when it rains.
Just the same
   I doubt I'll ever go there on a Sunday.

SEATTLE

I'd like to be a lumberjack again
stradling high trees
        instead of high-born women.
Climbing heavenward among the branches
out of the well of meaningless words
I've fallen into from too much city living.

Trees are monuments to God
            cities monuments to man.
I need to meet my god again
among the ferns and trees.
There's too much *me* in my life now
and not enough of *Him*.

And so I'd like to be a lumberjack again.

ATLANTIC CROSSING

I gave up airplane praying a while back.
I'd done the yellow beaches and the bars.
Written songs enough to keep my family safe for years.
Had some women that I liked and learned from,
                                    some I didn't.

My animals could live in luxury
I'd miss them more than they'd miss me,
                        but they'd be taken care of.
So if it came for me the way it did for Doug
there wouldn't be much left undone.
I'd have painted almost every picture
that I started out to paint.

I'll admit
there were some eyes I'd caught
that I'd have liked to keep.
But all in all I felt that I was ready
so I didn't pray on airplanes any more.

God hadn't frightened me for years
the way He first did
          when I'd run down His private fields.
We'd done some playing in the sky together
and if we weren't on equal terms
          I felt we had respect for one another.

Then you came running in my life.
                    I grew an inch.
And now while coming home to you
I pray until the seat-belt sign goes off
                    and then I pray again.

God let me live another day
to see you framed in any doorway
                    one more morning.

Don't let it happen on an airplane ride
when for that instant while I look at death
I might by chance forget the color of your eyes.

FOR BIMBY

Some things you cannot put down in a new way.
Sheep grazing on the airport road from Rome.
Stale February days and Bimby's smile.

Balloons never look like clouds to me
                              or crackerjack surprises
            or anything but just balloons.
So it is with Bimby's smile held in the Roman day
ablaze with waking tourists and sleeping cats
and ruins being ruined by the tick of time.

Her smile is just her own without elaboration
lost in the Alitalia afternoon.

CANNES

Cannes waking
in the winter morning
blue jackets sweeping down
the palm-lined street
and the empty bottles going back
to the empty-bottle places.

As jackhammers
do crossword puzzles
            on the sidewalk
and acrobats on painted yellow cranes
scoop out a new foundation
the stray cats crawl back under buildings
                to avoid the noise.

Jet time zones
still adjusting in our heads
we mix the shoes up
in the hotel hallway
and lose another day
by going back to bed,
thanking God for January mornings
          and café crème
along the coasts of France.

D

Thirteen Songs

for Arthur Greenslade

THE SINGLE MAN

I live alone
that hasn't always been
easy to do for just a single man.
Sometimes at night the walls talk back to me
they seem to say wasn't yesterday a better day.

Always alone
at home or in a crowd
the single man off on his private cloud
caught in a world that few men understand,
I am what I am, a single man.

Once was a time
I can't remember when
the house was filled with love
but then again it might have been
imagination's plan to help along the single man.

I'LL NEVER BE ALONE

From your arms I'll make a wall
then I'll never be alone
I'll let your arms encircle me
when the nighttime comes.

From your smile I'll build a wall
the tallest wall that man has known.
Then I'll hide behind your smile
and never be alone.

Then we'll go gentle in the wood
and what we do for one another
will be warm and good.

I'll wear your love as one might wear
a crown of laurel in his hair
and then if you'll be there
I'll never be alone.

WHERE ARE WE NOW?

You brought me lilacs on my birthday once
that should have been enough
but sometimes gentlemen need stronger stuff
a turning of the head, a knowing smile in bed.

I buy you necklaces you never wear
to show how much I care
I might as well have brought you bouquets of thin air
for crystal beads can't fill a woman's needs.

And where are we now, where are we now?
A thousand miles apart.
What have we now, what have we now?
Not even love enough to break each other's hearts.

Is there some turning in the road we've missed
that's brought us here like this
taking each other like the dying take a kiss
our smiles are frowns that pull each other down.

Here comes the night again to cover up the day
and take your face away
the sum and substance of a lifetime that we've made
is nothing now as the day begins to fade.

And where are we now, where are we now?
A thousand miles apart.
What have we now, what have we now?
Not even love enough to break each other's hearts.

SOMMERSET

Every day was Sunday
and every month was May
and every girl who came along
was sure to come your way.
How many years ago was that
ten, fifteen or more
when we lived at Sommerset
in that time before?

That time before we grew so big
before we grew so tall.
Before our eyes were wide enough
to see beyond the wall.
How many years ago was that
it seems so long ago
when we lived at Sommerset
and watched the summer go.

There's a cold wind coming
I can tell.
Blowing back the memories
of times we loved so well.

When we lived at Sommerset
a life or so away
every day was Sunday
and every month was May.
How many years ago was that
ten, fifteen or more
when we lived at Sommerset
in that time before?

SILENCE IS GOLDEN

If I had a pistol to hold in my hand
I'd hunt down and silence the Good Humour man,
I'd pour sticky ice cream all over his wound
and stop him forever from playing that tune.

For silence is golden on a soft summer day.
It's a pity to let strangers take it away.

If ever I get me a license to kill
I'll war on the jukebox and jackhammer till
the wind and the rain rust up all their parts
and the worms and the woodchucks dissect their hearts.

For silence is golden and hard to be found,
and killed far too often by the jackhammer's sound.

If diesels and dump trucks and gossips were words
I'd feed them like kernels of corn to the birds
and then all the thumping and bumping and pounds
would come out forever like pretty bird sounds.

For silence is golden and soft as a tear.
The soft sound of empty is the next voice you'll hear.

BLESSINGS IN SHADES OF GREEN

Jack Frost, isn't it something
something to be seen
the long tall grass waving in August
blessings in shades of green.

Jack Frost, soft in the morning
things aren't what they seem
a long time coming, a long time going
blessings in shades of green.

If I could fly I'd never sail
I'd trap the moon above the water in a pail.

Jack Frost, where have you gone to
with your midnight dream
didn't you promise to turn me on to
blessings in shades of green?

THE WORD BEFORE GOOD-BYE

What is the springtime after all?
Only the other side of fall.
Oh, if I could have
I'd have made you a sunny sky.
Hello's the word before good-bye.
Sometimes it rains, sometimes it shines
yet the things I want are seldom mine.

How much of summer can we hold
before we turn and find we're old?
The things our mirrors tell us are all lies
Hello's the word before good-bye.
Sometimes it's dark, sometimes it's fair
yet when I go home at night
nobody's there.

Perhaps the next wind that blows in
will bring you back to me again.
Till then remembering just makes me want to cry,
Hello's the word before good-bye.
Sometimes you lose, sometimes you win
yet I can't forget what might have been.

SOME OF THEM FALL

Some of them fall like snowflakes
in the winter chill.
Some of them fall with no sound at all
and just roll down the hill.

Some of them fall like acorns
in the forest dense,
strung on a line of steel so fine
that makes a barbed-wire fence.

And some of their names are Eddie
and some of their names are Joe;
I can't say why some of them die . . .
that's not for me to know.

Some of them fall like raindrops
on a summer day,
there in a ditch the poor and the rich
with hardly a chance to pray.

Some of them fall like seagulls
off in a foreign land,
the blood from their cuts
the life from their guts
spread over the silver sand.

And some of their names are Peter
and some of their names are Bill—
I don't know why some of them die,
I guess I never will.

IT'S RAINING

It's raining
and the children splashing in the mud
and the old men darting in the doorways
and the lovers underneath umbrellas
                         don't seem to mind.

It's raining
see the leaves go flying past the window
we can sit inside and just do nothing
wouldn't it be nice to touch each other
                         gently, gently.

It's raining
like the tears of angels down the window
if we wait there's sure to be a rainbow
I'm here now, don't be afraid of thunder
                                        any more.

It's raining
I can't hear the crickets any longer
do you suppose they're drowning in the gutters
I don't think you love me any more
                                        at all.
And it's raining.

THE LAST OF THE WINE

I lie here dying in a hundred small ways
from voices crying my name down nameless hallways
and the clock keeps ticking—eating up the time
and I'm down to the last of the wine.

My stomach growling at the movement my hand makes
in reaching out toward the disappearing handshapes
and the room keeps turning slowly in my mind
and I'm down to the last of the wine.

And I crawl on my belly through the night
and I dream of dying in the sunlight.

As unseen shadows in the morning start to harden
I rise up singing to the angel in my garden.
Some dark and different angel of another kind
and I'm down to the last of the wine.

And the angel never taught me to pray
and I die with the dying of the day.

I'VE SAVED THE SUMMER

I've saved the summer
and I give it all to you
to hold on winter morning
when the snow is new.

I've saved some sunlight
if you should ever need
a place away from darkness
where your mind can feed.

And for myself I've kept your smile
when you were but nineteen,
till you're older you'll not know
what brave young smiles can mean.

I know no answers
to help you on your way
the answers lie somewhere
at the bottom of the day.

But if you've a need for love
I'll give you all I own
it might help you down the road
till you've found your own.

RUSTING IN THE RAIN

The old gate is rusting in the rain
and children coming home from school
no longer skim their pebbles
on the old town creek
that just around the bend becomes a pool.
And we've all grown older
come see where we have been
out here rusting in the rain.

The old house is creaking in the rain
and lovers coming down the hill
no longer stop to linger
by the old dead tree
they took away for lumber to the mill.
And we've all grown older
come see where we have been
out here rusting in the rain.

The old world is dying in the rain
and summer coming every year
no longer stops to wonder
as it goes along its way
did anybody ever live here.
And we've all grown older
come see where we have been
out here rusting in the rain.

LONESOME CITIES

There's a few more lonesome cities
that I'd like to see
while the wine of wandering
is still inside of me.

There's a few more pretty women
that I'd like to know,
a bridge or two I'd like to cross
a few more oats to sow.

Maybe when I've done it all,
seen all there is to see,
I'll find out I still cannot
run away from me.

But as long as trains keep runnin'
a restless man I'll be,
and there're a few more lonesome cities
that I've yet to see.